THE SALTWATER CROCODILE

BY COLLEEN SEXTON

BELLWETHER MEDIA • MINNEAPOLIS, MN

Jump into the cockpit and take flight with Pilot Books. Your journey will take you on high-energy adventures as you learn about all that is wild, weird, fascinating, and fun!

This edition first published in 2012 by Bellwether Media, Inc.

No part of this publication may be reproduced in whole or in part without written permission of the publisher. For information regarding permission, write to Bellwether Media, Inc., Attention: Permissions Department, 5357 Penn Avenue South, Minneapolis, MN 55419.

Library of Congress Cataloging-in-Publication Data

Sexton, Colleen A., 1967-
The saltwater crocodile / by Colleen Sexton.
    p. cm. – (Pilot books: nature's deadliest)
Includes bibliographical references and index.
Summary: "Engaging images accompany information about the saltwater crocodile. The combination of high-interest subject matter and narrative text is intended for students in grades 3 through 7"–Provided by publisher.
ISBN 978-1-60014-669-5 (hardcover : alk. paper)
1. Crocodylus porosus–Juvenile literature. I. Title.
QL666.C925S49 2012
597.98'2–dc22   2011014595

Printed in the United States of America, North Mankato, MN.

080111   1187

CONTENTS

An Attack in the Night

Andrew Kerr, his wife Diana, and their baby were camping with friends on the northern coast of Australia. The group pitched their tents about 150 feet (46 meters) from the beach. Early one morning, the couple heard a thud. Diana looked outside their tent and saw a huge saltwater crocodile staring back at her. It had left the water and wandered up to their campsite.

As Andrew sat up, the crocodile lunged at him and clamped its jaws on his legs. Andrew shouted to his wife. Diana tried to pull him free and screamed his name. The crocodile dragged both of them out of the tent and toward the beach. Andrew pushed and punched the crocodile, trying to free himself from its deadly jaws.

Another camper, 60-year-old Alicia Sorohan, heard the screams and rushed to help the couple. She jumped on the 14-foot (4-meter) crocodile's back. She punched its head, stabbed its eyes, and kicked its body. The crocodile let go of Andrew, leaving him with a broken leg and arm. It whipped its head backward and crushed Alicia's nose and teeth. It grabbed her arm with its jaws, nearly tearing it in half.

The crocodile dragged Alicia toward the water. Alicia's son, Jason, came running with a rifle and shot the crocodile in the head. The crocodile died before reaching the water. Andrew and Alicia were lucky. Victims rarely survive once a saltwater crocodile pulls them into the water.

After the Attack

Five years after the attack, Alicia Sorohan visited the campsite where it took place. Park rangers gave her the skull of the crocodile responsible for the attack. Alicia says she is still fascinated with crocodiles, even after one tried to take her life.

Killer Reptile

Saltwater crocodiles are one of the most dangerous animals in the world. These predators live in Southeast Asia and northern Australia. "Salties," as they are often called, swim in rivers, swamps, and along coasts in search of prey. They spend most of their time in the water, but they can also get around on land. Crocodiles travel by sliding on mud or crawling on their bellies. When they're up on all four legs, some saltwater crocodiles can run as fast as a human.

Long-Distance Swimmers
Saltwater crocodiles are excellent swimmers. They often swim as far as 600 miles (970 kilometers) to find and claim territory.

Australia

saltwater crocodile territory =

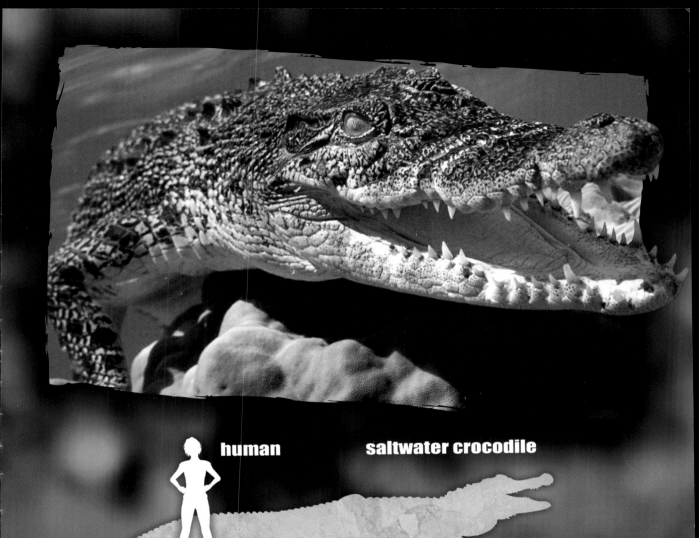

human   saltwater crocodile

Saltwater crocodiles are the largest **reptiles** in the world.
They can grow to be 20 feet (6 meters) long and weigh more than
2,000 pounds (900 kilograms). Covered in oval-shaped **scales**,
their dark, rough skin is **camouflage** in muddy water. Their short
legs end in feet with sharp claws. Saltwater crocodiles sweep their
long, muscular tails back and forth to swim. They also use their tails
to launch out of the water and attack.

Saltwater crocodiles have long, flat heads that are built for hunting. Their eyes, ears, and nostrils sit on top. This allows crocodiles to sink down in the water with only a small part of their heads showing. Salties can float this way for hours, waiting for prey.

Saltwater crocodiles will dive down deep to search for underwater prey. Most dives last about 15 minutes, but the largest crocodiles can stay underwater for two to three hours. A second set of eyelids slides into place when saltwater crocodiles are completely underwater. These clear lids protect the eyes and allow crocodiles to see their prey. A flap of skin behind the tongue seals the **windpipe**. The flap keeps water out when crocodiles open their jaws to attack.

Around 65 million years ago, crocodiles roamed Earth with dinosaurs. Crocodiles survived when dinosaurs died off. This may be because crocodiles were well adapted to their environment. They could go a long time without food, survive in cold weather, and recover from bad injuries. Today's crocodiles have changed little from their ancient ancestors.

and hold on to prey. Salties close their jaws with tremendous force. They apply a pressure of 2,000 pounds (900 kilograms) per square inch. Victims who have survived an attack say it feels like getting hit with a hammer. Together, the jaws and teeth tear the flesh and crush the bones of a victim.

The skin around the jaws has **sensors** that help saltwater crocodiles find prey. Anything that disturbs the water sends out **pressure waves**. The sensors detect those waves and guide crocodiles toward their prey.

A Deadly Grip

Crocodiles have the most powerful bite of any animal on Earth. Their bite force rivals that of the Tyrannosaurus rex.

swim. They burst out of the water and seize their prey at a speed of up to 18 miles (30 kilometers) per hour. The average saltwater crocodile ambush lasts less than a second! Crocodiles then drag their prey underwater. They toss their heads back and forth and go into a **death roll**. They spin around, drowning their prey and tearing them into bite-sized pieces.

Upset Stomach?

Strong acid in a crocodile's stomach helps it digest prey quickly. Crocodiles also swallow rocks to help grind up food in their stomachs!

dailes take down wildebeests, crush turtle shells, and snatch fish as they swim by. Their strength, speed, and **instincts** make them one of the fiercest predators on the planet. They will eat just about anything, even humans.

Surviving an Attack

In the mid-1900s, people hunted saltwater crocodiles. They made shoes, belts, and purses out of the skin. The number of saltwater crocodiles decreased throughout Southeast Asia and Australia.

In the 1970s, Australia made it illegal to hunt salties. Since that time, the saltwater crocodile population has grown quickly. In 1971, between 3,000 and 5,000 saltwater crocodiles lived in Australia. Today, 100,000 to 150,000 salties swim in the country's waters. Crocodiles are now wandering into places where people live. The number of attacks on humans is on the rise.

Smart Predators

Saltwater crocodiles have good memories. They know where and when schools of fish will migrate. They also remember the locations of campsites and hiking trails.

Salties will attack people if they feel threatened. Every crocodile has its own territory that it fiercely protects. Salties may see humans as invaders. Female crocodiles also defend their nests. If people get too close, females will attack to protect their eggs and young.

The best way to avoid an attack is to stay out of a crocodile's reach. Anyone who sees a crocodile should get away from the water as quickly as possible. People should never go swimming in areas known to have crocodiles. They should also stay away from the water's edge. Crocodiles are drawn to the smell of food. People should never clean fish near the water or leave food scraps out at a campsite. Campers should set up their tents far from the water. Boaters need to be careful, too. Dangling arms or legs could invite salties to attack.

19

Attack Facts

- An estimated 20 to 30 saltwater crocodile attacks happen every year. Less than half of them are fatal.

- The number of saltie attacks may be greater. It is thought that many attacks occur in areas where they are not recorded.

Saltwater crocodiles depend on their ability to sneak up on prey. It's difficult for a victim to escape once he or she is taken, but it is not impossible. Victims have fought off crocodiles by stabbing them in the eyes or punching their nostrils. Hitting the back of a crocodile's mouth breaks the seal over its windpipe. The crocodile releases its victim to save itself from drowning.

Some groups are working to reduce saltwater crocodile attacks on humans. When crocodiles are sighted in areas populated by people, these groups capture and move the animals. One of the best ways to avoid saltwater crocodile attacks is to stay away from their territory. Once they sneak up on you, it only takes a second before you're in the most powerful jaws on Earth!

Glossary

camouflage—coloring and markings that hide an animal by making it look like its surroundings

death roll—when a crocodile holds prey in its mouth and twists around in the water to confuse and drown it

instincts—behaviors that come naturally

pressure waves—waves of energy that can travel through air, water, earth, or other materials; for example, sound waves are pressure waves.

reptiles—cold-blooded animals that have backbones and lay eggs to produce young; reptiles have scales and move on their bellies or short legs.

scales—plates of skin that cover and protect a reptile's body

sensors—body parts that receive signals and respond to them; saltwater crocodiles have sensors that detect the presence of prey.

windpipe—the tube through which some animals breathe; the windpipe runs from the throat to the lungs.

To Learn More

At the Library

D'Ath, Justin. *Crocodile Attack*. Tulsa, Okla.: Kane Miller, A Division of EDC Pub., 2010.

Hamilton, Sue. *Attacked by a Crocodile*. Edina, Minn.: ABDO, 2010.

Snyder, Trish. *Alligator & Crocodile Rescue: Changing the Future for Endangered Wildlife*. Richmond Hill, Ont.: Firefly Books, 2006.

On the Web

Learning more about saltwater crocodiles is as easy as 1, 2, 3.

1. Go to www.factsurfer.com.

2. Enter "saltwater crocodiles" into the search box.

3. Click the "Surf" button and you will see a list of related Web sites.

With factsurfer.com, finding more information is just a click away.

Index

The images in this book are reproduced through the courtesy of: Mike Parry/Minden Pictures, front cover, p. 9; Photoshot, pp. 4-5; Andy Rouse/Getty Images, pp. 6-7; James D Watt/ imagequestmarine.com, pp. 10-11; Jean Paul Ferrero/Ardea, pp. 12-13; Newspix/Rex USA, pp. 14-15; Jeff Rotman/naturepl.com, p. 17; Doron Aviguy/Rex USA, pp. 18-19; Ian Waldie/Getty Images, pp. 20-21.